The Essence of The Bhagavad Gita

Nirmala Raman

Qurate
quratebooks.com

The Essence of the Bhagavad Gita
Nirmala Raman

Published in 2025

© Published by

Qurate Books Pvt. Ltd.
Goa 403523, India
www.quratebooks.com
Tel: 1800-210-6527, Email: info@quratebooks.com

ISBN: 978-93-58988-14-7

Dedicated to my beloved

husband, "Hullo Mister"

Your presence will be missed ,

but your spirit will always guide me.

THE BHAGAVAD GITA

All in One and One for All

PREFACE

The Vedas and Upanishads are the glorious, ancient Indian philosophical texts, while The Ramayana and The Mahabharata are the two greatest Indian epics written around 5000 years back. The Bhagavad Gita forms a small part of the Mahabharata, and is of very great significance, as it contains the essence of many of the Upanishadic Truths.

The Bhagavad Gita is not a book for any particular religion, but a Universal Guide to Righteous Living. It shows you how to face the challenges in life, how to empower yourself, and a thousand other things. It may be called an **"All in One and One for All"** book. Though the main characters, Lord Krishna and Arjuna are from the Hindu religion, it must be remembered that they are just symbolic names to represent the Higher Force and the common individual.

The inevitable Mahabharata war took place in Kurukshetra between the cousins- Pandavas and Kauravas. Arjuna, the Pandava prince, a great warrior, had to fight for justice, against his cousins, the Kauravas, for regaining their ancestral kingdom of Hastinapura. Being a great devotee and friend of Lord Krishna, Arjuna arrived at the battlefield, with Krishna as his charioteer. Reality struck, as he saw his beloved teachers, his grandsire and all his kith and kin, with whom he had to fight. He became dispirited, despondent and depressed. He could not bear to think of killing any of them in the battlefield, and, totally disheartened, laid down his arms. Lord Krishna then gave him the historical advice in 704 verses (The Bhagavad Gita), and enlightened him about life and death. From a confused and dejected man groping in the darkness, Arjuna becomes a bold and enlightened individual, ready to face the challenges of life. This Immortal Bhagavad Gita, is very relevant even today. It can be treated as the Gospel for humanity as a whole, to dispel his ignorance and darkness and ignite knowledge and enlightenment . There is an Arjuna in each one of us, who can become enlightened by The Divinity (Krishna) within us.

The Bhagavad Gita is an Immortal Ocean. What I have attempted to do is just offer a cursory glimpse into this profound vastness of knowledge and wisdom. I have just tried to give the reader a cupful from this ocean in the fond hope that the thirst for more and more will goad him on to read the original text and its various deeper interpretations by our numerous revered spiritual masters.

Today's generation is so busy with the stress and strife of modern living that even if they wanted to, they are unable to find time to delve into the great gems of our exhaustive spiritual texts. I have penned this condensed piece to fill this genuine need and enable such people to get at least a basic idea of such texts. To a great extent, the contents of this book have been gleaned from the various lectures and writings by spiritual leaders like Swami Chinmayanandaji, Swami Tejomayananda, Swami Tapasyanandaji, Swami Parthasarathy and others. I am eternally grateful to them.

"Some books are to be tasted, others to be swallowed, and some few to be chewed and digested," said Sir Francis Bacon. I sincerely appeal to the reader to include this book in the last category.

May you all stay Blessed and successfully face life's challenges.

OM TAT SAT

Contents

Play you well, the game of life
Be you free from stress and strife.

INTRODUCTION

The Bhagavad Gita was written by sage Veda Vyasa more than 5000 years ago. The contents are applicable even today because it is a science. It predates all religions and hence cannot just be called a holy book of the Hindus. It is a guide to living. It teaches us the goal to be attained and the way to achieve it. It not only shows us how to face the challenges of life but also reveals who we truly are- Our True Self. Shri. Adi Shankara extricated the 704 Gita verses from the Mahabharata and gave them to us.

In the Mahabharata war between the cousins, the Pandavas and the Kauravas, a confused, disillusioned, and dejected

Pandava, Arjuna, lays down his arms and refuses to fight, as it would amount to killing his kith and kin and even his respected teachers. The Lord enlightens him and finally, from a confused, agonized, and disillusioned Arjuna, he is transformed into an enlightened Arjuna, ready to fight and face the challenges of life. This transition from Darkness to Light, from Ignorance to Knowledge, from an Absolute No to an Eager Yes, from Escape and flee to Stand and boldly face, from Negativity to Positivity, is the crux of this great treatise.

The Bhagavad Gita is a symbolic representation of the eternal war within us. It symbolises the constant fight between our divine impulses (the good, represented by the Pandavas) and negative tendencies (the bad, represented by the Kauravas). The spark of Divinity within each one of us, guiding us throughout life, in the form of a soft voice from within, is The Great Lord Krishna/Higher Consciousness/ Awareness/ Our Higher Self.

It should also be remembered that throughout the Bhagavad Gita, the Lord represents the True Self- the Awareness or Life Principle in each one of us, while Arjuna represents the common self - the confused, shattered human being, who has become so because of his internal maladjustments. Thus, in a sense, we have within us, both the Divine Principle (Lord Krishna) and the mere Mortal Principle (Arjuna).

The Bhagavad Gita is in the form of a Q & A session between Lord Krishna, the charioteer and His disciple, Arjuna on the battlefield of Kurukshetra. (Sanjaya, the minister, who is blessed with divine vision, narrates the whole episode taking place in the Kurukshetra battlefield to the blind king Dritharashtar, father of the Kauravas.) Throughout the Bhagavad Gita the reference to man is at all his three levels- body, mind, and intellect- BMI.

(Important Note: The entire expounding of the Bhagavad Gita by Lord Krishna is done in a rare moment of His Yogic

Integration when He is totally identified with the Higher Self or Divine Principle that is pervading everywhere. Hence whenever he says "Me or Myself" etc, it is to be regarded as the Declaration of Divinity and not to be construed as the bragging of a mere historical personality, a mortal Krishna, the child of Devaki. It is something like electricity declaring "I am the one energy that gives the glow in all filaments!)

Fear and Escape are for the weak
Face the challenges and forward leap.

CHAPTER - 1

VISHADA YOGA

(The Yoga of Arjuna's Despondency)

(Escapism)

This chapter describes all the warriors assembled on the battlefield and shows Arjuna's despondency and dejection at the thought of having to fight and maybe even kill his teachers & cousins. Seeing in person, his own grandsire, the grand old Bhishma who was more than a father to him, his loving teacher, Dronacharya, his cousins, the Kauravas, Karna, and many others, his heart sank. He laments and tells Krishna ' What pleasure can I get after killing my own kith and kin ? Even if I should gain the kingdoms of the earth and all the kingdoms of the three worlds, it will not give me any pleasure. Whether I win or lose,I cannot rejoice. I do not want this kingdom or war'. Thus, unable to confront the challenge, he decides to cast aside his bow and run away from the battlefield.

Thus ends the 1st Chapter of the Bhagavad Gita entitled 'the Yoga of Arjuna's Despondency'.

OM TAT SAT

The Atman is Real, the rest is illusion
Get up and fight and be not in delusion.

CHAPTER - 2

SAANKYA YOGA

(The Yoga of Knowledge)

(Face the Challenges of Life)

This chapter can be taken as an epitome of the Bhagavad Gita. To dispel Arjuna's delusion, the Lord explains:

1. All of us have within us an Eternal Spirit or Atma, which is but a Spark of the Divine. We should learn to associate ourselves with the Atma, rather than think of ourselves just as a mere physical, mental, or intellectual being. The Atma never dies. Nor can it be slain. This body passes on from childhood to youth and then to old age and finally death. The cells have all changed. But there is one thing which has remained constant and changeless throughout,and this is the Divinity, / Atma / Awareness/ Consciousness / Life Principle which enables everything in us and the entire cosmos. After death, which is mandatory for whoever/whatever is born, It (the Divine Principle within us) just passes onto another body, to

be reborn again and continue the cycle of life and death. Thus, The Lord convinces Arjuna that no one can kill the Eternal, Immortal Reality (Atma) within, and what he might have to kill is only the mortal self, which, anyway, has to die one day.

2. By not meeting the challenges and running away from the battlefield, he is only failing in his ordained duty. As a Kshatriya, his karma or primary duty was to fight for his country, and against injustice. Symbolically, this is also a Divine call of the Lord to man- to discard his fears in the face of life's challenges, and to come forward to play his ordained role in the game of life, as best as he can.

3. The Lord then gives an extraordinary description of how work has to be performed. Working in one's chosen field is a MUST! No one should try to shun it. Work should be done with a single-pointed devoted mind to the best of your ability, irrespective of the rewards and recognition. *(Many skeptics may find this absurd; but the truth is that this is the most profound statement ! Let us examine this : Work done with the expectation of the fruits will only result in stress and anxiety. There is bound to be disappointment, as there are so many outside factors involved in granting the rewards and recognition. But, when we work just for the sake of work, there is bound to be more perfection in the work as we will be free of unnecessary anticipation, fears, and doubts about the results/ fruits.)* This is true Karma Yoga, and this alone will lead to spiritual awakening.

4. A very valuable piece of advice is given on the inner attitude that we should have while executing our duties or transacting in the world. Equanimity of mind is very important. Pain/Pleasure (relating to our intellectual zone), Loss/Gain (relating to our mental zone), and Conquest/Defeat *(relating to our physical zone) are integral*

parts of life. Learn to treat them both equally, trying not to be affected too much by them. (Initially, it may be tough, but at least we can begin by not becoming overly joyful or sinking too low with dejection when pleasure or pain comes.)

5. The qualities of a STITHA PRAJNYA, a man of steady wisdom are also clearly enumerated. He completely casts off all desires from his mind, is blissful in his own experience of the Self, is neither shaken by adversity nor gloats during prosperity, is free from attachment, fear, and anger, meets life with equanimity during good and bad times, neither rejoices nor hates, can withdraw his senses from the sense organs and objects, and their mad lustful wanderings in their respective fields, and focus attention on the Highest.

6. The control of the mind. Initially, it might seem very difficult. But in reality, we have been doing this throughout our lives. Our attachment to toys (in childhood) was overcome when we got attached to computer games. Similarly, this attachment waned when we got attached to some friends, etc The secret is that when we get attached to a higher, the lower always falls off. This is a law. Hence when we get attached to the Highest, all other lower tendencies will automatically drop. This is the key.

7. Another great guidance given by the Master : Be very aware of your **thoughts!** This is the seed that can make or mar us. It has a powerful cascading effect. Encouraging a single harmful thought, can soon create havoc ! It can sprout to a seemingly harmless material desire, for example, then progress as an attachment, followed by a Burning Desire for possessing and enjoying it. It leads on to Anger(if the desire is not fulfilled) or Greed (when the desire is fulfilled), then Delusion, and finally, even loss of Discrimination. It's a Lose - Lose Situation. Hence, one

has to constantly watch the mind and train it to live in self-control, while moving among the sense objects, with neither an attachment nor aversion to them. (Of course, one can thoroughly enjoy the rightful sense objects in the world, in moderation. But let the enjoyment be as long as the physical contact is there. It is the hankering after or craving or the hangover effect that brings harm). When you practice self-control, you get great Peace of Mind which in turn leads to Happiness. Happiness is = number of desires fulfilled divided by number of desires harbored. For more happiness, we may increase the numerator, but more importantly, decrease the denominator!

Thus ends the 2nd Chapter of the Bhagavad Gita entitled, 'The Yoga of Knowledge'.

OM TAT SAT

Work is Worship, an offering Divine
Actions selfless make them sublime.

CHAPTER - 3

KARMA YOGA

(The Yoga of Action)

(Work is Worship)

This chapter is extremely relevant in today's world. It teaches us the invaluable lesson of Action or Work, and how it is to be performed.

The question arises - is work or action really necessary? Certainly yes! Action is a MUST. It is our basic nature. Our bundle of vasanaas (mental impressions and desires) with which we were born has to be exhausted by our actions. This is because vasanaas continue to stick with us and manifest and shape our personalities in our future births, thus preventing us from true liberation/Moksha/Self Realization. Sri Ramana Maharishi had often stressed the importance of removing vasanaas for self-realization. This exhaustion of the vasanaas can be accomplished only by the good, unselfish actions or work performed in this world. Hence action is mandatory.

Now, How should we act? The uncultivated man acts thoughtlessly, propelled by his wrong tendencies and sensuous desires. These may initially give fleeting joys, but ultimately give only endless sorrows and inexhaustible vasanaas. The **right action** is God-dedicated selfless actions performed in a spirit of devotion and surrender. This will not add to your vasanaas. Any type of action can become a glorious "sacrifice" only if it is undertaken and performed with purity of motive, deep surrender, and intense love. This is what is meant by WORK IS WORSHIP.

Two Basic Aspects of Right Action are :

1. Generate Energy. This can be done by surrendering the mind i.e. your likes and dislikes, focusing the intellect on the Divinity within us, and making the physical body act dynamically.

2. Avoid dissipation of energy. This can be done by not having worries about the past, not being anxious about the fruits and results of the future, and excitement about the present.

The Basic Steps for Right Action are:

1. Dedicate all your actions to the Lord, following His teachings with devotion and without Doubt.

2. Act in accordance with your inner tendencies .Things will become easier as you already have the potential for it.

3. Act dynamically, without attachment (expectation), worries of the past, or hopes and anxieties of the future. There should be objectivity, a disinterested interest in action. Otherwise, it will be like driving a car with brakes on.

4. Try to become more and more unselfish in your actions. i.e. act with just the feeling that 'it's my job to do this and I must do it to the best of my ability'. Then forget about it. Only self-centered actions give us stress and strain.

5. Work without being too bothered about a reward - materialistic (money), emotional (praise, fame), or intellectual (acceptance of your ideas). This alone will benefit you. Otherwise, you would be looking for fulfillment and happiness from outside which may or may not come! (Both are harmful. If it comes from outside, it may lead to greed, and if it does not, it may lead to frustration, anger, etc.). Moreover, when anxiety creeps in, you cannot put your best into the present action.

6. Work should be done as an **enjoyment**. This can be achieved only if you have the right value for things. A higher value for any work can be achieved when you shift your thinking from 'I have to get more money and recognition for this work', to, 'It's my job. Let me do my best, and enjoy it'. If you are a teacher, enjoy the smile on the faces of your students, when they learn something new, or sometimes place you even on a higher pedestal than their own parents ! If you are a doctor, enjoy the relief you give to a suffering patient ! If you are an artist, think of the joy you give to your audience - in almost all the ways, work can be done as a joy and fulfillment. It can be its own reward and a great source of joy. And above all, since there is greater focus on the job alone, it will result in the best outcome.

7. Let the Intellect/ Buddhi/ the power of discrimination guide you and NOT the senses or emotions. The mind is always wandering, having lots of likes and dislikes. Subdue it with the discriminatory power of the Intellect. Verse 7 gives a complete technique of right action. "Controlling the senses by the mind, engage the organs of Action in KarmaYoga, without attachment".

Controlling the senses is the most difficult and of course, the most important task. But, this is the **only way** to throw overboard the greatest enemy of mankind- **desires..** Material desires are harmful either way, whether fulfilled or unfulfilled. When fulfilled, they give rise to greed, arrogance, envy, and fear of losing- causing great confusion of mind, loss of intellect, and final destruction. If unfulfilled, they give rise to anger, disappointment, and delusion. Desires are born only because of our Spiritual Ignorance. Once we realize our TRUE SELF, through the process of Meditation (where we withdraw ourselves from our false sense of identification with the objects, the body, mind, and intellect, and calmly repose in our True Divine Self), we end our ignorance and thus kill our desires. No more than can these desires, even if they arise in the mind, play havoc with our inner lives.

Thus ends the 3rd Chapter of the Bhagavad Gita entitled, 'The yoga of action'.

OM TAT SAT

Serve them well, those in need
In every man, there's God indeed.

CHAPTER - 4

GYANA YOGA

(The Yoga of Knowledge)

(Right Knowledge Makes Every Act a Worship)

The Blessed Lord declares that He, although of an unborn and imperishable Nature, manifests Himself in every age. Whenever there is a decay of righteousness, He manifests in this world to re-establish goodness and destroy wickedness. He also declares that if one can free himself from attachment, fear, and anger and absorb himself in Him (The Supreme Being), the final goal is assured.

Continuing on the topic of Action, the Lord says, 'Action is the insignia of life'. It's not **what** you do in life that matters so much as **how** you do it. A person hardly praying or going to temples, but not having hatred and enmity towards others is a greater devotee (bhakta) than one who prays and visits temples a lot, but still nurtures envy, hatred and enmity towards others. Play your part in life, just like an actor on stage, giving your best shot.

Remember that the Real You (Your Divine Principle) is **not** the limited person you are now. Try to constantly remind yourself of it. Actions of the Enlightened are not binding, since they are free from desires, expectations, and attachments, and are even-minded in success or failure.

Every action can be done as an offering of worship to the Divine. Throughout our lives, all our actions can be converted to become a Yagna (ritual sacrifice). Right Knowledge makes every act a Yagna. Using the metaphor of the most familiar Vedic ritualism at that time, where oblations were offered into the sacred fire to invoke the Blessings of the Deities, there is a description of 12 Yagnas. When some materials are offered into a sacred fire, not only are they consumed by the fire, but a Great Blessing ensues.

The 12 Yagnas are:

Yagna of action: Whatever becomes your activity, give it your Best. Use it as a means to the final goal of discovering Yourself. **Yagna of Individualities:** Nothing is done for a limited purpose, but for everyone's welfare. **Yagna of perception .Yagna of restraint** i.e Self Control. **Yagna of Senses and Vital airs;** Wealth, Physical Services, Emotions & Ideas, Study & Wisdom, Pranayama, and Inner Strength to outer activities. **Yagna of Jnana or Knowledge:** This Yagna of Knowledge is far superior to materialistic offerings or mere formalistic ritualism. In this, man renounces all his ignorance into the fire of Knowledge kindled by him which consists of 2 aspects i.e. Negation of the False (the wrong notion that we are just this limited false mortal self) and Assertion of the Real Nature of the Self (our true Divine Self). To acquire this, you should have the Intellectual attitude of Surrender, the Mental Aspect of Enquiry, and the Physical aspect of Service. It is this fire of Knowledge that reduces the actions to ashes i.e. removes the Vasanaas. This knowledge of Reality, Our true Eternal Self will carry you from the Shore of Mortality to Immortality and protect you from the shocks, agitations, and worries of the world to the harbor of Peace and Bliss.

The surest way of acquiring Wisdom:

1. Start with the Physical body by subduing and controlling the senses. Controlling the senses does not mean self-denial, since this will only be a repressed desire and will soon return. Self-control is when you fix a target and ensure your actions are taking you towards it.

2. Proceed to the Mind, with devotion, giving undivided attention to the path of self-development.

3. Finally to the Intellect by developing Shraddha, the ability to be consistent and dedicated intellectually.

(The difference between Knowledge and Wisdom- Knowledge is found in books . But, when this knowledge is lived practically in life, it becomes Wisdom)

The man who is thus full of faith, and devotion and has subdued the senses obtains this Knowledge. Conversely, he who has neither the knowledge of the Self (at least a clear intellectual understanding even if not a Spiritual Realization) nor Shraddha, the intellectual readiness to grapple with and understand the Scriptural declarations, or even if he is a Doubting Thomas, doubting the Self, he will not find happiness anywhere. Our Blissful Nature / Our True Self is revealed only by our Self-effort.

Thus ends the 4th Chapter of the Bhagavad Gita entitled "The Yoga of Knowledge".

OM TAT SAT

Do your duty with smile and cheer
Of the results, have no fear.

CHAPTER - 5

KARMA YOGA

(Communion Through Renunciation)

(Work With Detached Attachment)

In answer to Arjuna's doubt whether a life of action is better than that of contemplation, the Lord replies that both are equally valid paths. However, unless the path of dedicated and detached action is undertaken first, the second (the path of contemplation, characterized by abandonment of all actions), cannot happen. It will only lead to idleness and hypocrisy.

Great importance is given to detachment or renunciation in action. Renunciation does not mean a life of denial or giving up things that are dear to you. It only means growing, and appreciating the far more fulfilling avenues of enjoyment. It is an exhilarating confidence in the higher aspects of life. Again, it does not mean giving up on actions but acting in a spirit of renunciation. This alone will lead you out of bondage to liberation, where you are not impaired by the BMI. (Body, Mind, Intellect). When 'good' things come your way, enjoy it by all means, but do not develop a craving or attachment towards it. *(For example, if you have a sweet tooth, by all means relish and enjoy eating them in a limited way. But do not have a great craving or excessive desire for them to the extent of spoiling your health.)* Know where to draw the line, and draw it. It is the excessive desires and cravings that are man's greatest enemy. Learn to eliminate or at least reduce them, to get back to your **infinite stature and power**. "A person who is established in selfless and dedicated action, who is pure, and whose mind and senses are under control, and whose self is identified with the self of all, he is never bound," says the Lord.

What is the BEST way to perform actions?

1. Remove the arrogance of **ego** from your actions. Do not be proud that "I am doing this..." Do not have the doership attitude. Realize that it is the Atman, which is the source of all actions, and which enlivens even the simplest of actions; and it is the vasanaas (inherent tendencies) that determine the nature of the actions. Constantly remember to attach yourself to the Higher Self, the Atman. Remember, we live in the body but we are **not** the body. Even temporarily, if you switch from body awareness to mind awareness, like a student writing his last answer in his exam, or an artist deeply engrossed in his art, the physical pain is non-existent. How much more beneficial would it be to attach ourselves to our Real Self - The Atman!

2. Dedicate your actions to something higher, setting aside your selfish interests and desires. Be ever ready to serve. When you put someone or something ahead of you, it gives you tremendous power. The more self-centered the action, the more will be the problem. Eg. A teacher, doctor, or lawyer should focus on what is good for the students, patients, or clients rather than how much money or fame they will make. This may be difficult initially but can be achieved with steady determination. It is

the Law of Nature that when you hold on to something higher, the Lower automatically drops off as seen in your own life - childhood (toys); youth (cellphones/friends), adulthood (money/power); old age (spirituality)! Thus, train yourself to constantly raise your actions to a nobler cause (a higher cause). Automatically, the lesser (selfish & self-centered) cause will drop off.

3. Do actions without clinging to a motive or reward. Learn to get fulfillment in doing an action just for the sake of doing an action. This is **not** an idealistic philosophy but a very practical and beneficial one. Do action for the sake of doing the action. Do even your obligatory duties with the attitude that that's what you ought to do. It has multiple benefits. Your concentration is **only** on the action and will turn out excellent, as it has no worries about the rewards and is not hampered by prejudices of the past or fears and expectations of the future. There is no dissipation of energy in negative thoughts or anxieties. Remember clearly that the fruit of your action is Never in your hands. It is always dependent on someone else. And you have no control over that. Hence there is bound to be disappointment and even frustration when **your** expectations are not satisfied by others. By all means, fix a goal, work to the best of your ability, and let your conscience get the satisfaction. Work like an artist who just enjoys his work of art- be it painting, writing, or singing. His work is his Reward! What matters then, how the world looks at it ?!

Another important aspect in this chapter is the development of **one-ness** with everyone. This can happen **only** when you realize that you are a Spark of the Divine, by attaching yourself to the Atman Principle in you, and later on extending this same idea to all beings in creation.

The last verse gives the prescription for liberation. It says "Excluding all sense perceptions, fixing the look between the eyebrows, steadying the flow of Prana and Apana (outgoing and incoming breath) through the nostrils, controlling the senses, mind and intellect: devoid of desires, fear and anger- the meditative sage attains liberation.

Thus ends the 5th Chapter of the Bhagavad Gita entitled "Karma Sanyasa Yoga Yoga Of Renunciation of Action".

OM TAT SAT

Meditate on 'Who' you are

Realise your Divinity- 'That You Are' .

CHAPTER - 6

DHYANA YOGA

(Yoga of Communion Through Meditation)

(Raise your Lower Self by your Higher Self - Meditate)

Arjuna's original plan was to escape from the battlefield and live a 'sanyasi life'. The Lord clarifies that a truly selfless worker alone is the greatest sanyasi. The inert mind **has** to be first stirred into intense activity. Then it has to be trained. This chapter deals with the technique of training and cultivation of the mind.

Doing actions (yoga) and doing them in a detached way (sanyasa) are the 2 sides of the spiritual coin. Sanyasa is the State reached through Yoga, the Practice. Thus, rituals or religious practices Do have an initial place in Spiritual Development. But they are only a means and not the ultimate goal. When a man ceases to have any attachment to all the objects of the senses and actions and renounces all thoughts of the world, he becomes a Yogi.

We should raise our lower self, consisting of our body, senses, and mind, by our Higher Self, consisting of the Atman /Divine Spirit in each one of us. The wandering, wavering sensuous mind (the sole cause of the lower Satanic self in us) should, under the guidance of the intellect, (which is the equipment for the Higher Self to manifest) be disciplined and made to attune with the nobler Divine Self in us. Such a self-controlled serene individual, who constantly contemplates on his true Self, becomes an unshakeable Yogin. To him, pleasure and pain, honor and dishonor, heat and cold, friends and foes are all equal. This Highest Goal can be reached only by Meditation, a Spiritual Communion.

How to practice Meditation?

1. Sit in solitude i.e. withdraw from mental and physical preoccupations and retire to a quiet corner of the house. Sit comfortably in a clean place, on a seat that is neither too high nor too low.

2. Self- Controlled- body and mind controlled i.e. freeing oneself from the eagerness to possess or hoard.

3. Make the mind one-pointed by subduing mental imaginations and activities of the sense organs and contemplating on the Ultimate Self.

4. Sit in an erect posture- head neck and vertebral column erect and perpendicular to the seat, holding the body firmly and relaxed. Keep your eyes half closed, gazing at the tip of the nose or the space between the eyebrows.

5. Always be moderate in eating and sleeping habits and firm in the vow of Brahmacharya- i.e. all sense impulses. Keep the mind serene, fearless, and balanced.

Thus keeping the body and mind, fix the concentration on the Atman/Brahman/Self.

This has to be practised tirelessly, with determination, under the guidance of a steadfast intellect. Thoughts will come. The intellect should be used to curb them and bring the mind back to abide in the Self. Of course, the mind is fickle, turbulent, and unyielding, but the Lord assures that it **can** be brought under control.

A true Yogin / a man of spiritual insight can easily experience the Infinite Bliss of contact with the Brahman and soon sees the Self as residing in all Beings, and all Beings as residing in the Self.

Arjuna wants to know what would happen to that person who has firm faith but is not steadfast in his practices and hence fails to reach Spiritual Perfection. The lord assures: "NO SPIRITUAL PRACTICE GOES IN VAIN". The fallen yogi goes to the spheres of Righteousness after death, and after the specified time, is reborn in this world, in an environment (pure, wise, and spiritual families) conducive to his spiritual growth. He will regain the spiritual discernment of his previous birth and strive harder for that perfection!

Thus, this is a sure path of Peace, leading to bliss and attaining Moksha or Liberation. The Yogi then attains that quietude of mind, becomes steadfast, never moves from Reality, and reaches that Ultimate State, free from feeling any pain, sorrow, or other agitations of the mind - a permanent transcendental Bliss!

Thus ends the 6th chapter of the Bhagavad Gita entitled Communion through Meditation.

OM TAT SAT

Wisdom is gained by guarding the senses,
The mind, the intellect and the impulses.

CHAPTER - 7

GYANA VIGYANA YOGA

(Yoga of Communion Through Knowledge and Realization)

(Matter and Spirit- Prakriti and Purusha)

The Lord explains that He manifests at two levels- the lower, Prakriti, (the 8 fold material nature, which is His Unconscious Nature), and the Higher, Purusha (spiritual manifestation as Jivas or Centres of Consciousness). Prakriti evolves into various spheres and Species of Beings so the Jivas reap the fruits of their Karma and gradually evolve into perfection to become one with the Divine. Thus each individual has these two natures of the Divine (Prakriti and Purusha) as his source. Once the individual understands this distinction, he will realize that the Spirit, identified with matter, is the root cause of all sufferings. But when the Spirit becomes detached from this identification with matter, It rediscovers Its own essential Nature as Bliss/Absolute/Divine. This should be our most important aim in life.

What is Prakriti? The Prakriti is 8-fold, consisting of Earth, Water, Fire, Air, Space, Mind, Intellect,and Ego.The outer world of stimuli reaches the **5 sense organs** which then transmit them to the inner point of focus- **the mind.** The stimuli are then rationally systematized by the **intellect**. At all these levels of sense perception, mental reception, and intellectual assimilation, there is a continuous sense of one-ness; this is called the **Ego.**

What is Purusha? The Purusha is the Spiritual entity/ The Divine Spark within each of us, which is Pure Consciousness or Awareness, and which maintains, nourishes, and sustains everything.

The Lord then goes on to describe Himself - the Divine Element. He is the Essence of all entities, manifesting their characteristic Nature and Function. He is the Origin and Dissolution of the entire Universe- the taste in water, the Brilliance in the Sun, the syllable OM in all the Vedas, the fragrance in the earth, the righteous desire (that desire unopposed to Dharma), etc. The three gunas of Maya -Satwa, Rajas, and Tamas all arise from Him. The Lord clarifies that though the Gunas proceed from Him, He is in no way controlled or contaminated by them - just as the waves are in the Ocean, but the Ocean is not affected by the waves. Unfortunately, most men are deluded and do not understand the True Nature of the Divine.

The Lord then explains that there are 4 types of devotees- the sufferer, the enquirer, the boon seeker, and the knowing or wise one. Though all are considered noble and virtuous, the last one is dearer to Him because his love stems from his sense of Innate Unity with the Lord, and hence unmotivated and constant. They make no demands or expectations and carry only themselves as their offerings in a pure spirit of love inspired total surrender. The only cry in their heart is to end the separation and be made one with Him. Those people whose wisdom is blinded by various desires adore other deities and perform various forms of worship. And whatever form any devotee desires to worship with faith, that faith is made firm and unflinching by the One Lord alone. The fruit however is only temporary. In contrast, worshippers of the Supreme Reality i.e. Seekers of the Self, discover themselves and become One with the Self/ Divine.

From their very birth, all beings are deluded by the bewitchment of the pairs of opposites- arising from desires and aversions. The only way we can rediscover our equipoise as the Eternal Self is to arrest, control, and win over the agitations of the mind. The virtuous man, freed from the pair of opposites, (pleasure or pain, likes or dislikes, etc) worships the Lord with great steadfastness. Such a true meditator, meditating upon the Self, comes to realize his identity with the Conscious Principle in himself-his True Divine Self

He becomes a man of Realization, understanding the vagaries of the mind, the nature of all activities, and the world of objects. He will continue to be aware of that Reality and even at the time of death will have his mind ever absorbed in the Supreme Divinity.

Thus ends Chapter 7 of the Bhagavad Gita entitled The Yoga of Knowledge and Wisdom- Jnana Vijnana Yoga.

OM TAT SAT

Control your thoughts, be not its slave

Become its master, bold and brave.

CHAPTER 8

AKSHARA BRAHMA YOGA

(Yoga of the Imperishable Brahman)

(The Cosmic Cycle: Pitru Loka and Brahma Loka)

This chapter describes the Lord, the Cosmic Cycle, and the means to achieve Moksha. Explaining the Divine Mystery, the Lord says that He is the Supreme Imperishable Brahman and His inherent nature is what manifests as the indwelling spirit, the creative act which brings forth all beings into existence, the great elements, and His presence in them as Purusha, guiding their evolution. A brief description of the Cosmic Cycle (manifestation and dissolution) is given. The periods are spoken of as the day-time and night-time of Brahma, the Lord of Creation. 1 human year = 1 day of the celestials; 1200 such celestial years make 1 chaturyuga (4 yugas). 1000 chaturyugas make 1 day time of Brahma (Kalpa) and an equally similar period is His night (Pralaya). 365 such days and nights make 1 year of Brahma. A hundred such years constitute His life span. The end of His life span is marked by a major Pralaya (Maha Pralaya) of duration equal to his lifetime. After that, the creative cycle (Maha Kalpa) starts again. Thus, the Infinitude of time is depicted. Thus, the course of the cosmic cycle is that the whole universe comes into manifestation from the Unmanifest (Prakriti) at the dawn of the day of Brahma and dissolves in that Unmanifest itself when the night of Brahma begins. But the Supreme Unmanifested state remains unaffected and this Imperishable state is the Supreme Abode of the Lord. When attained, one cannot be reborn anymore. This should be the Ultimate Goal.

The Lord then describes 2 paths - 1. The path of sure–return. Also called the path of the Ancestors (Pitrayana). He who lived a lifetime doing good deeds and performed rituals (karmas) unaccompanied by any worship (Upasana), after death, goes to Pitruloka (Heaven). After his merits gained by his good actions are exhausted, he will return to his deserved embodiments, ordered by his individual vasanaa balance. Smoke, night time, the dark fortnight, and the six months of the southern solstice of the Moon, the presiding deity of the sense enjoyments, indicate the Path of the Ancestors. 2. The path of no-return. Also called the path of Gods (Devayana). He who lived a lifetime doing good, performed rituals (karmas) and worship (Upasana) will walk this path and entering through the Sun, will go beyond it to Brahmaloka, enjoy Bliss till the end of the cycle, when they, along with the creator, get total liberation. Fire, flame, daytime, the bright fortnight, and the six months of the Northern Solstice of the Sun indicate the Path of the Gods. Thus, one leads to Samsara and the other to Moksha. The Lord gives a firm assurance that whoever leaves his physical body, thinking of Him alone will undoubtedly attain Him. But for this, along with the prescribed duties, one must constantly think of Him. With the syllable OM (His sound symbol), draw your mind inward and meditate on Him.

Thus ends the 8th chapter of the Bhagavad Gita entitled AksharaBrahma Yoga or The Yoga of the Imperishable.

OM TAT SAT

Anything offered with devotion and love
Is far more precious to the Heavens above.

CHAPTER - 9

RAJA VIDYA RAJA GUHYA YOGA

(The Yoga of Royal Knowledge and Royal Secret)

(Divinity - Your Essential Nature)

Look up to Him, You will reach Him!

The Spiritual Science enunciated in this chapter is the Science of the Self- the deepest essence in each individual. Knowing this can free man from the cycle of samsara and ensure his union with the Lord. It should be remembered that throughout the Bhagavad Gita the Lord represents the *Higher Self*, the Awareness or Life Principle in each one of us, while Arjuna represents the common, confused, shattered human being, the *lower self*, who has become so because of his internal maladjustments.

Lord says that the entire world is pervaded by Him/Self/Awareness, the Unmanifested Being. All objects exist in Him and He is the Source and support of everything. He pervades everything but He does not dwell in them - just as all the waves are contained in the Ocean, but the Ocean is not contained in the waves. As the mighty wind, moving everywhere, rests in space, all Beings rest in Him. This Absolute Reality is All inclusive- Viswathomukam- the sacrifice, the worship, the ancestral offerings, the father, the mother, the grandsire, the sustainer, the syllable OM, the 4 Vedas, the goal, the support, the refuge, the friend of all, the heat, the rain, the mortality, the Immortality, and the Substratum of the entire Universe. This Eternal Brahman, functioning through the total mind is the God Principle, the Creator. And the same Brahman, functioning through the limited individual mind and intellect is the Individualized self, the mortal ego. The same sun gets reflected in the clear still waters of a vast lake and the disturbed muddy pool, in different ways. Similarly is the difference of the same God Principle in different Beings. Thus the Lord is the vital animating Reality behind the Creator and also behind the Created.

At the end of the Cosmic cycle (Pralaya), all beings resolve into Nature (Prakriti), which is also His own, and at the beginning of a new one (Kalpa), get projected. However, these activities do not bind Him, as He remains detached- no attachment or aversion, and His actions are neither egocentric nor desire-motivated. He is only a Sakshi or a witness. Unfortunately, foolish men do not understand His true essence and mistaking the idol for Reality, become deluded, resulting in fanaticism. But great souls seek the Immortal by realizing the Self through single pointed Self-application. They worship the Ultimate Reality in a steadfast, continuous way, filled with devotion, always performing selfless activities in a spirit of yagna.

Those seekers, well versed in the Vedas and rituals, performing sacred acts of devotion and sacrifice with a desire to enjoy celestial Bliss, will certainly get their wish and enjoy the pleasures of Heaven, but after the credit of their merits has been exhausted, will again continue the cycle of births and deaths. But, those who just love and serve the Lord without any selfish desire or motive (even for salvation), will merge and become One with Him.

(Though external worship is needed in the initial stages since a beginner needs some object of worship, it is to be remembered that it is only symbolic). The true and Highest form of Worship is the Total offering of oneself- one's possessions, actions, and even the sense of agency (I am doing this). True worship does not have to be an elaborate or expensive affair. The Lord clarifies that a leaf, flower, fruit, or even water will suffice. What is needed is great love and devotion. The inner mental attitude is more important. Whatever you do, do it as an offering to the Divine, with love and dedication. An unparallelled statement! In this way, all our actions can become offerings to the Divine, and life itself can become a sanctified noble one. The Lord assures that such men will be freed from the bonds of actions and shall attain Him. Real Bhakti is practised through constant remembrance and contemplation of Him. This will ensure that everyone- irrespective of class, color, sex, and even sinners will attain God Realisation.

Thus the Lord's Sovereign Secret is "Fix your mind on Me (that Immutable Self), be devoted to Me, sacrifice to Me, bow to Me, and having thus united your whole self with Me, taking Me as your Supreme Goal, you shall come to Me."

Thus ends the 9th Chapter of the Bhagavad Gita entitled "Raja Vidya Raja Guhya Yoga" or The Yoga of the Sovereign Science and Sovereign Secret.

OM TAT SAT

Turn your mind a little Inward
Feel the magic of rising Upward.

CHAPTER - 10

VIBHUTI YOGA

(The Yoga of the Divine Glories)

(Describing the Indescribable)

Arjuna wants to know more about how one can constantly keep in touch with the Eternal, even while transacting with the world. Hence a more detailed account of the Lord's Divine glories is enlisted.

He is the source of all, unoriginated, and knowing Him fully, man becomes free from delusion. All the higher faculties of man - intellect, wisdom, non-illusion, forgiveness, truth, self-restraint, calmness, equanimity, contentment, happiness, pain, fear, fearlessness, fame etc. - arise from Him alone. The seven great sages are just the thought projections of Him. The person aware of the manifold manifestations of His being (Macrocosm) and His Divine Powers (Microcosm) become established in Him.

The Lord assures those people who serve Him wholeheartedly and are ever steadfast in loving communion with Him, that he will reside within him, (as his innermost self), destroy his ignorance, and show him the path of reaching Him.

In answer to Arjuna's further doubt as to how to constantly contemplate the Lord in worldly terms, Lord Krishna enumerates a whole list of more than 75 forms of His creation and on how to meditate individually and intensify one's integration. What a mind-boggling list! Some of them are: Among the 12 Adityas, He is Lord Vishnu; among the Luminaries-Sun; Vedas-Saama; Senses-mind; Peaks/Mountains- Meru; Words OM; Sacrifices-Japa; Devarishis-Narada; Cows-Kamadhenu; Beasts-Lion; Birds Garuda; Sciences-Science of the Spirit (Spirituality); Immovable things Himalayas; Warriors- Rama; Water- Ocean; Sarpas (single-headed snake)- Vasuki (adorns Siva's ring finger); Nagas (multi hooded snake)- Anantha(the 1000 hooded snake- Lord Vishnu's bed); Weapons- Vajra; Metres- Gayatri; Months - Margasirsha (dec15 to jan15); Yadavas-Vasudeva; Pandavas-Arjuna; Sages Vyasa; Things Sacred- Silence and Seasons-Spring. He is also the Wisdom of the Wise, the Splendor of the Splendid, and the Seed of all Beings.

The Lord concludes since the human mind cannot comprehend the vast magnitude of the Divine , the purpose of the enumerations is only to draw man's attention to just a faint reflection of the Divine so that man can turn his outward going mind inward and contemplate on Him.

Thus ends the 10th Chapter of the Bhagavad Gita, entitled Vibhuti Yoga or The Yoga of the Divine Glories.

OM TAT SAT

Away from attachments- they only Bind
Freed from desires, peace you will find.

CHAPTER - 11

VISHWAROOPA DARSHANA YOGA

(The Yoga of the Vision of the Universal (Cosmic) Form)

(Vision of the Divine Magnificence)

(This chapter is considered to be a very auspicious one as the Lord bestows a great Blessing to Arjuna (and incidentally, Sanjaya) by revealing His Vishwaroopa or His Cosmic form.)

In answer to Arjuna's humble request, the Lord decides to demonstrate His earlier theoretical description by practically revealing His Glorious Form. He grants Arjuna the Divine vision to behold His Viswaroopa (Magnificent form), as the normal vision cannot perceive it. Sanjaya, the narrator of the battle, along with the blind king, Dritarashtra, is the only other lucky person who was blessed with this special vision.

Initially Sanjaya and later on Arjuna himself describes the Indescribable Majestic Splendour of the Lord. Sanjaya reports to King Dritarashtra "having countless faces and features, bedecked with countless celestial ornaments, robes, and garlands, equipped with countless divine weapons, having the brilliance of a thousand suns - there, in the body of the Lord, Arjuna saw the whole Universe, resting in one, with all its infinite parts- a multiplicity being unified in His being". Arjuna's words " I see all the Gods in your body and also hosts of various classes of beings. I see your all-encompassing form everywhere with myriad arms, trunks, eyes, without a beginning or end, diademed and armed with weapons. I see you infinite in the Power of endless arms, the sun and moon being your eyes, your mouth heating the whole universe with your radiance. The space between earth and heaven is filled with you alone. Into you, enter these hosts of Devas, and sages and celestial singers extol Thee with sublime hymns. The Vedic deities like Adityas, Visvas, Maruts, and Siddhas all view Thee in utter amazement. The whole world is trembling with awe at your stupendous form, touching the sky and flaming in many colors. All those on the battlefield are rushing headlong into Thy fearful mouth. I have lost my sense of direction and am terrified. Please return to Your original form and tell me who Thou art and Thy purpose here." Even with the special vision, Arjuna's eyes are bedazzled and he is unable to perceive anything more. Thus, after Blessing Arjuna with a quick darshan of His Vishwaroopa, The Lord returns to his original form.

The Lord then explains that He is the mighty world-destroying Time, now engaged here in annihilating all beings and that even without Arjuna, none of these warriors would live. He then tells Arjuna to arise and fight, and do his duty (as a Kshatriya), and reinstates that he is just an instrument of the Lord. Arjuna once again sings the praises of the Lord, saying that He is indeed the Ultimate haven of rest and safety for all the worlds, and that He is the Primal God, by whom the entire Universe is pervaded. He begs forgiveness for not having realized His greatness and regarding him as a mere friend, and again requests Him to come back to His original form. The Lord then explains that the Universal Cosmic form was revealed only to Arjuna and it could not be seen by others. He asks him not to be bewildered or afraid and to behold once again the great Vision. He then assumes His gentle form, as Arjuna's charioteer.

The Blessed Lord then declares that this Form of His (which even the gods are longing to behold) cannot be easily seen by the study of Vedas, rituals, austerities, or sacrifices. Only by single-minded devotion can one know, see, and reach Him. "He who does actions for Me, who looks upon Me as Supreme, who is devoted to Me, who is free from attachment, who bears enmity towards none, he comes to Me " is the promise given by the Lord Himself!

In the last 2 verses of this chapter, the Lord, as the perfect teacher, summarizes the important points of how to attain Moksha.

The seeker first, through God-dedicated activity, learns to withdraw his attachments from other things and then turns his mind to devoted attachment to the Lord. The God Principle alone becomes his goal and automatically other finite attachments with the world of objects will gradually disappear, resulting in his coming into contact with the Self. Having become the Self, he will then recognize himself everywhere and in everything and so there cannot be enmity towards anyone.

Love for all and hatred for none is the Geeta Motto for Spiritual growth.

Thus ends the 11th Chapter of the B.G entitled the "Vishwaroopa Darshana Yoga" or the Yoga of the Divine Cosmic Form.

OM TAT SAT

Joy and Pain, treat them the same
Treat your life as a beautiful game.

CHAPTER - 12

BHAKTI YOGA

(The Yoga of the Path of Devotion)

(Qualities of a true Devotee)

This is a unique chapter of the Bhagavad Gita, and is usually taught first, especially to young children, as it is very simple to understand. It also gives a broad list of all the good qualities that we should try to strive for.

The practice of devotion: The Lord declares that though both the Manifested (seeing Him in a known form) and the Unmanifested (the Eternal Form) forms of worship would yield the same result, the former is easier for the man of body consciousness. He says "Fixing the mind on Me, worship Me, ever steadfast, self-controlled and with Supreme Faith." Worship the Lord, regarding Him as the Supreme goal, meditating on Him with single-minded devotion, and renouncing all actions in Him i.e acting as a messenger of the Lord , without the arrogance of 'I am the doer'. When you renounce your actions to a Higher Power, you end your limitations and identify yourself with that Power. Once you fix your mind and intellect on the Lord, you will live in Him alone. If you are unable to steadily fix the mind, pursue the Yoga of constant practice i.e. whenever the mind wanders, gently bring it back with the help of the intellect. If even this is not possible, perform actions for His sake. If even this is difficult, then, taking refuge in the Lord, self-controlled, renounce the fruits of all actions. (Note: The fruit of an action is the action of the Present moment, maturing in a Future period. When the negative imagination of a future is not there, the present action will be more dynamic, single-pointed, and effective.) Knowledge is better than spiritual practices, and Meditation is better than Knowledge, but the best is when one renounces the fruit of one's actions. This will ensure immediate Peace, says the Lord.

The Lord then enumerates 26 qualities of a true devotee :

1. Has no hatred towards any creature.
2. Is friendly and compassionate to all.
3. Is free from attachments. (possessions).
4. Is free from egoism (arrogance).
5. Is balanced in pleasure and pain.
6. Is forgiving.
7. Is ever Content.
8. Is steady in Meditation.
9. Is self Controlled.
10. Possesses firm conviction.
11. Has a devoted Mind and Intellect, and dedicated to the Lord
12. Will not create agitation or fear in anyone.
13. Is ever peaceful with himself and not agitated by the world.

14. Is free from the moods of joy, envy, fear, and anxiety.
15. Is free from wants, pure, alert, untroubled, and renouncing egoism in all undertakings.
16. Neither rejoices, nor grieves, nor hates, nor desires.
17. Renounces good and evil.
18. Is full of devotion to the Lord.
19. Has the same attitude to friend as shown to foe.
20. Has the same equanimity of mind in honor and dishonor (intellectual), cold and heat (physical), pleasure and pain (mental) i.e. at all levels remains unagitated, as he is free from attachment.
21. Has the same attitude towards censure and praise.
22. Is silent.
23. Is content with anything.
24. Is homeless- i.e. free from all sense of possession and mental shackles.
25. Is Steady-minded, steadfast in his spiritual goal.
26. Is full of devotion.

Concluding the enumeration of the various moral, ethical, and spiritual qualities of a true devotee, the Lord declares that those who follow the Immortal Dharma (Sanatana Dharma), endowed with faith and regarding Him as their Supreme Goal, are exceedingly dear to Him.

Thus ends Chapter 12 of the Bhagavad Gita, entitled Bhakti Yoga or the Path of Devotion.

OM TAT SAT

Spirit and Matter are what you are

Know them well before you 'Cross the Bar'.

CHAPTER - 13

KSHETRA-KSHETRAJNA VIBHAGA YOGA

(The Yoga of the Field and its Knower)

(Free yourself from your Bodily Identification)

This is one of the most famous chapters, as it explains about our true self, free from the material associations. The matter equipment and their perceived world of objects constitute the Field (Kshetra) and the underlying Supreme Consciousness illuminating them, the Knower of the Field (Kshetrajna). The knowledge of the distinction between the two alone is True Knowledge.

This body is called the Field (Kshetra) It consists of the 5 great elements (earth, fire, water, space, and air), the egoism (I-sense), the intellect, the Vasanas or Unmanifested(i.e the Avyakta, that which rules the functions of a given mind and intellect, and determines their activities in the world outside), the 10 organs (5 sense organs of perception-eyes, nose, ears, tongue, and skin and 5 sense organs of action-hands, feet, mouth, rectum, and genitals), 5 objects of the senses (see, hear, smell, taste, and touch), and the mind. Apart from these 24 factors, modifications like desire and hatred, pleasure and pain, the assemblage of the body, intelligence, and steadfastness are also included in the Kshetra.

The Supreme Consciousness, called the Knower of the Field (Kshetragnya), cannot in reality be described in words. Still, for our understanding, He can be thought of as facing all directions, having hands and feet everywhere, and eyes, ears, and mouth grasping everything. He is the transcending Spirit, enveloping all that exists in the world, both moving and nonmoving, within and without all beings, the Generator, Supporter, and Devourer of all Beings, seated in the heart of all. This Supreme Self is without a beginning or end, and is devoid of qualities. Even though it dwells in all beings, it neither acts nor is tainted. Just as the sun illumines the whole world, good or bad, the Atman, (i.e the Supreme Self), illumines. It is only a Sakshi (witness).

Continuing further, the Lord explains: Prakriti (Matter) and Purusha (Spirit) are 2 aspects of the Lord. All the changeable objects of the attributes that constitute the world of daily experiences are sprung from Prakriti. Prakriti is the cause of the formation and functioning of the body and the senses, while Purusha is the cause of the experience of pain and pleasure. Seated in bodies, which are the products of Prakriti, the Purusha experiences the objects and qualities born of Prakriti. Attachment to these objects and qualities born of Prakriti is the cause of his (Purusha or Spirit) embodiment in good and evil wombs. Purusha has no samsara. But when It identifies with the Kshetra (Prakriti), it becomes the experiencer. He identifies with the body and senses, which are the effects of Prakriti. Wherever any being is born, moving or unmoving, it is due to the union of Kshetra and Kshetrajna. He who sees the Supreme Lord existing equally in everything reaches the highest goal. In this body there is also The Supreme Purusha, the Transcendent, unconcerned Witness, the Great Lord. Prakriti alone is the cause of all actions. The Self or Atman itself is actionless just like electricity manifesting itself in fans, lights, fridges, etc., or petrol, manifesting itself in cars, scooters, or buses. Though they are the cause for the functioning of the fans, cars, etc. they are not responsible for its performance or otherwise. This depends solely on the nature of the fan, car, etc.

To be able to perceive this discrimination and attain true knowledge, certain prerequisites are required by the seeker: Humility, unpretentiousness, noninjury, forgiveness, uprightness, service to the teacher, purity, steadfastness, self-control, indifference to the objects of the senses, absence of egoism, the ephemerality of life, nonattachment, distaste for crowded society, constant and unswerving devotion to the Lord, constant application to spiritual texts and disciplines, and a clear comprehension of the goal of spiritual enlightenment.

In conclusion, the Lord assures that whoever perceives the distinction between Purusha and Prakriti and of the liberation of the Spirit from the hold of Prakriti by spiritual insight, meditation, the discipline of knowledge or work, worship, or from instructions from teachers or elders, reach the Supreme.

(Note: Swami Chinmayananda says, "He who has realized 1) that which is matter, 2) that which is spirit, 3) how the Spirit, deluded by its pre-occupations, gets identified with matter and behaves as Kshetrajna (knower of the field), and 4) the mysteries of the gunas, under the influence of which the equipments function, becomes a man of wisdom.")

Thus ends Chapter 13 of the Bhagavad Gita, entitled Kshetra Kshetrajna Vibhaga Yoga or the Yoga of the Field and Its Knower.

OM TAT SAT

Satwa, Rajas and Tamas, your actions colour

Watch these Gunas and guide them ever.

CHAPTER - 14

GUNATRAYA YOGA

(The Yoga Of The Gunas)

(We are what we are because of Our Three Gunas)

This chapter tells us a very important truth - the science behind our behavior and that of others.

The Spirit functioning through matter is responsible for and expresses itself as the individual who lives his experiences in this world.

The Universe is evolved by the Union of Spirit and Matter. The Great Nature (Prakriti) is like a womb, in which the Lord has placed the seed of His creation. Thus, all creatures have originated from the same womb (Prakriti) and the same seed (Purusha/the Supreme Consciousness). However, of the innumerable varieties in creation, no two individuals, even of the same species, are alike. This is because the Purusha (the Supreme Consciousness) seated in Prakriti (Matter), experiences the Gunas, born of Matter. Gunas refer to the attitude with which the subtle body- the mind- functions and not to the properties of the material. The psychological being in every one of us comes under the influence of the 3 different gunas - Sattwa/Purity, Rajas/Passion, and Tamas/Inertia - which makes us act the way we do at any given moment. All 3 gunas are present in everyone, but their proportions differ, which is why individuals behave differently. Once an individual can recognize the various influences under which he is forced to function from time to time, he will be able to discard all wrong and immoral tendencies in himself. *Not only that, he will also be able to empathetically understand the behavior of others. And this is extremely important.*

Sattwic Guna: is luminous, stainless, and harmonious due to its essential purity. When the mind is under its influence, it is steady and free from evil thoughts. It binds by attachment to Happiness and Knowledge. Thus, when we efficiently and intelligently become aware of the world and judge it correctly, Sattwa is predominant in us.

Rajasic Guna: expresses itself through Passion. When there is an onslaught of Rajo Guna, the mind is wrecked with many painful passions expressed in a million different urges like desires, emotions, feelings, etc. The main sources of all these fall under two categories - desires and attachments. **Desires** for the acquisition of things and the creation of situations that are expected to give some personal happiness and the sense of a **clinging attachment** to things already acquired. These two are the root cause of the strife and struggles to acquire, possess, and guard. It goads man to act endlessly, earning and spending, saving and procuring. Rajas is predominant in us when we exhibit greed, activity, restlessness, longings, etc.

Tamasic Guna: is born of ignorance. Under its influence, man's intellect gets veiled and he becomes incapable of discriminating between right and wrong. There is no brilliancy of thought, tenderness of emotion, or nobility of action. He becomes indolent and heedless of the nobler and divine aspirations of life. When Tamas predominates, there is inertness, heedlessness, delusion, idleness, confusion of mind, inability to arrive at any decision, and a tendency to escape all responsibilities.

At any given moment, one predominating guna operates, while the other two, though still present, are not prominent enough to operate. All these gunas are not only effective in our present lives but continue even after death. Death is nothing but a total divorce of the subtle body, consisting of the mind and intellect, both of which are only a bundle of thoughts, from its physical structure. Hence, these tendencies of the mind have to be cultivated, developed, pursued, and strengthened in this life. There should be a constant striving to increase the Sattvic Guna , reduce the Rajasic and have a minimum of Tamasic Guna. The nature and number of desires and attachments are determined by the Gunas, and it is their (desires and attachments) quality and quantity that form the Blueprint of our next birth.

The Sattwic predominantly evolve upwards, Rajasic dwell in the middle, and the Tamasic go downward. However, total release can be had only when one can transcend all the 3 Gunas. The Spirit, identifying itself with the mind-intellect, dances to their mood determined by the gunas. To stand apart from the mind by ending all our identification with it is to get complete freedom from our thought processes. This is the aim of meditation.

When the Seer realizes 1. One's ego which was previously claiming to be the agent in all his activities is none other than the gunas themselves, governing and directing his thoughts at all times and in every one of us, and 2. That which is higher than the Gunas is Consciousness/Awareness itself, he becomes liberated.

Such a man neither hates nor longs for the effects of the 3 gunas i.e. remains in a state of equanimity, even when he feels agitated and deluded. He stays centered on the Self, and swerves not. To him, pain and pleasure, a clot of earth, precious stones, and gold are all alike. He has the same attitude in censure, praise, honor, dishonor, friend, or foe. No ego or ego-centric desires, possessing or hoarding will tempt him. To him, contemplation (as it can't be done all 24 hours) is coupled with dedicated service, i.e. working intelligently with God's Awareness. The Lord assures that such a person is sure to be liberated.

Thus ends Chapter 14 of the Bhagavad Gita entitled Gunatraya Vibhaga Yoga or the Yoga of the Gunas.

OM TAT SAT

He is a spark in you, as Purushotama
You are a part of Him, as Jivatma.

CHAPTER - 15

PURUSHOTTAMA YOGA

(The Yogaof the Supreme Spirit)

(Dispassion Leads to the Love and Knowledge of the Divine)

BEWARE OF YOUR VASANAS- THEY ARE THE BLUEPRINT OF YOUR NEXT BIRTH.

The spiritual concept in this chapter is shown through an allegory of the Pipal (Aswatha) tree. The eternal Aswatha, the World Tree, the cosmic tree,

Samsaravriksha, unlike other trees, has its roots in the Highest regions, signifying Brahman, and the branches in the lower regions, referring to the cosmic mind, egoism, 5 subtle elements. These are stated to extend downwards because as they go down they become grosser. Just as the leaves protect the tree, the Vedic Hymns protect the tree of the world. In the world of men, the branches spread into regions high and low, covered with leaves of sense objects and nourished by the gunas, (since gunas determine your leading a higher or lower life) and thus entangling man in the bondage of action. This tree of samsara, consisting of sense objects, gunas, vasanas, etc., can be cleft with the strong axe of detachment. And then, that Highest Goal, the Absolute State, the Supreme Abode from where there is no fear of return, should be sought after. Detachment to a lower goal can happen only when there is an attachment to a higher goal. To reach this goal, the seeker should be free of pride and delusion, have conquered attachment, be ever dwelling in the Self, have desires completely at rest, and be released from the pair of opposites like pain and pleasure.

The structure and nature of the Ego: The individual, undergoing experiences of birth and death is called Jiva- the Embodied Self. This Jiva is the Eternal Light of Consciousness, playing upon and seemingly conditioned by the subtle body constituted by the mind and intellect. The Eternal Self, having become a living soul in the world of life, and abiding in Prakriti (matter), draws to itself the 5 senses, with the mind for the sixth. Though the Infinite cannot be divided, the reference is just like space being called room-space and outer-space. It is this Spark of Consciousness that vibrates the entire body with life, renders existence possible, and maintains by its very presence the sense faculties and mental capacities. This Jiva takes to itself various bodies from time to time and incarnates in different environments which are ordered by its burning desires and aspirations. At death, the subtle body permanently departs from the gross physical body, taking along with it the faculties or fragrance of the mind and senses, just as the wind takes the fragrance of the flowers. Thus viewed, the mind is only a bundle of vasanas (thought personality). And these vasanas can exist only in the Infinite Consciousness. Thus, the Infinite Consciousness illumining the vasanas is called the individual personality - the Jiva. This Jiva, through the equipment of the mind and senses, enjoys the objects of the world. Only the man of Realization, who can still his mind and keep his intellect free of disturbing attachments and desires can become aware of this.

The Lord's Immanence: It is the Divine Consciousness that illumines the entire world, shines in the radiance of the sun, moon, and fire, permeates the soil, supporting and nourishing all creatures by its vital energy, and associated with all the physiological activities. It is the Self, seated in all hearts. But, though the Infinite is present everywhere, He is most conspicuously self-evident in the Heart/Mind of the meditator during meditation. In philosophy, the term heart refers to the mind. He is Unconditional, All-pervading, and Eternal. He is other than the two Purushas in this world (the perishable purusha - bodies of all beings, and the imperishable purusha - jivatma or the embodied soul,) and is wholly beyond the perishable world of matter, pervading the three worlds of waking, dream and deep-sleep and thus called as Purushottama.

When man has fully identified himself with the Infinite Supreme, he becomes a true devotee, worshiping the Divine with all his being. Thus the Lord, reveals the Most Secret Science, the Brahmavidya, and declares that the man who knows this becomes a man of realization, and can henceforth not create any confusion and sorrow for himself or others.

Thus ends Chapter 15 of the Bhagavad Gita entitled Purushottama Yoga or the Yoga of the Supreme Spirit.

OM TAT SAT

Beware of Anger, Lust and Greed
The three sure ways to Hell indeed.

CHAPTER - 16

DAIVA ASURA SAMPAD-VIBHAGA YOGA

(The Yoga of the Divine & the Demonic)

(Three Gates to Self Destruction - Anger, Greed and Lust)

This chapter describes the qualities found in the basic 2 kinds of people. Those endowed with a divine nature (Deva) and those of a demonic (Asura) nature. Of course, no individual is entirely good or entirely bad.

Though Kshetrajna, the Absolute Consciousness, is the same in all Beings, each one's behavior and experiences are different. This is because of the Kshetra (individual bodies) being under the influence of the different gunas (temperaments).

The physical, mental, and intellectual behaviors when life pulsates through a disciplined body and an undisciplined body are described.

The divine traits in a cultured man living a spiritual way of life are Fearlessness (comes with knowledge), Purity of heart (seen in one's motives and intentions), Steadfastness in Devotion and knowledge (which can happen only when the mind is turned inward), Charity at the level of head and heart (includes sympathy, kindness, sharing - material things, knowledge, etc), Restraint of senses, Sacrifice, Study and practice of the scriptures, Asceticism, Tapas (all conscious restraints at the body level which help reduce the indulgences in the external world and increase the energy within), Uprightness, Ahimsa (at body and mental level), Truth, Even tempered, Spirit of renunciation (Thyaga), Quietitude (Shanti), Unmalicious Tongue, Love, Non-Covetousness, Gentleness, Modesty, Vigor or Tejas, Patience ((that subtle boldness shown when calmly facing even the most provoking situations), Fortitude, Forgiveness (remaining calm even in provoking situations), Non- hatred, and Humility.

On the other hand, the demoniac traits of man are Hypocrisy, Ostentation, Arrogance, Anger, Self- conceit, Materialism etc. These demoniac men are ignorant of what and what not to do, holding ideas of impurity and evil. Always wedded to anxiety and care, their only goal is the satisfaction of their lust. Because they are bound by hundreds of desires, they strive to obtain and hoard by unlawful means. Given to egoism, power, lust, anger, and haughtiness, these asuraic people are born and reborn in the same environment, and gradually sink lower to the very depths.

Showing the technique of hastening one's spiritual evolution, the Lord warns us to shun the 3 main gates to Hell (self-destruction) - Lust, Anger, and Greed. Lust is excessive desire. When not satiated, it leads to anger, and when satiated, leads to greed. Either way it's a lose-lose situation. Follow the guidance of the scriptures in doing what you have to do and avoiding what you should not. This is the way to reach the Supreme Goal.

This exhaustive list of good and bad has been reiterated towards the closing chapters so that mankind has a ready reckoner to refer to when he starts his introspection or self-analysis.

Thus ends Chapter 16 of the Bhagavad Gita entitled Daiva Asura Sampadhyudhi Yoga or the Yoga of the Divine and Demonic Types.

OM TAT SAT

"OM TAT SAT" - chant it oft
That alone can chasten your thought.

CHAPTER - 17

SHRADDHATRAYA VIBHAGA YOGA

(Yoga of the 3-Fold Faith)

(Your Preferences are Dictated by your Gunas)

The Lord, in this chapter, describes the faith with which the people of the 3 different types of gunas act in the various fields - Sattvic (pure- shows signs of clarity, self control, wisdom, harmony and balance), Rajasic (passionate- shows signs of egotism, ambition, activity, passion, and energy) and Tamasic (dark - shows signs of inertia, confusion, attachment, destruction and ignorance).

All human beings are endowed with the rare gift of Shraddha (Faith) just like reasoning power and other higher faculties. Faith is different from belief. While the latter is just a mere conventional acceptance of an idea, the former is stronger, as it puts into practice the accepted idea. It is the inner intuition and natural receptivity of the mind to the ideals. Now, the kind of faith he has depends on his three gunas. His preference with respect to worship, food, sacrifice, tapas or austerity, and charity depends on these gunas. The faith of everyone is according to his natural disposition (derived from his past impressions.) The Lord then describes the threefold faith in various things.

1. Worship: Sattvic people worship the Devas (Gods) for higher spiritual goals and noble qualities. It is performed as ordained in the scriptures, merely with the feeling that he must do so, without the expectation of the fruits. The Rajasic worship the Yakshas and Rakshasas (demigods) for money, power, fame, etc. The intention here is for the fruits and ostentatious, vain display. The Tamasic worship the ghosts and hosts of Bhutas for a vicious sense of gratification. These men of vain and senseless nature even practice terrific austerities and mortifications of the flesh, not enjoined in the scriptures, without sincerity, impelled by lust and attachment.

2. Food: Sattvic men have a natural taste for clean, wholesome, nourishing, and agreeable food that increases vitality and promotes happiness and cheer. The Rajasic prefer food having a strong flavor and dense taste - very hot, pungent, sour, salty, bitter, etc. The Tamasic desire stale, putrid, tasteless, and impure food like fermented drinks.

3. Sacrifice: That sacrifice which is offered by men without the desire for the fruits as enjoined by the scriptures, with a firm faith that it is his duty, and without the sense of doer-ship, is Sattvic. That sacrifice done for show and ostentation, with ego and with an eye for fruits /reward, even recognition, is Rajasic. Sacrifice done contrary to the scriptures, devoid of mantras or faith is Tamasic.

4. Tapas: The threefold austerity of the body, speech, and mind, practiced steadfastly, with no clinging attachment and no anxiety for the fruits is Sattvic Tapas. Austerity is not a life of brutal self-denial, but an intelligent way of living in the right relationship with the world, avoiding all unnecessary dissipation of our vital energies, and directing the conserved energies

to spiritual endeavors. It includes: a) The Physical - includes the worship of the Gods, the Brahmins who have realized the Self, the teachers, and the wise. The practice of steadfastness, Brahmacharya- contemplation of the Brahman is not possible unless we are away from our bodily sense objects and turn inwards to the Spirit, Non injury in all physical, emotional, and intellectual realms. b) Speech- Speech is a powerful vehicle in man and has to be used wisely. The words spoken should bring no disturbance to the others, be irritating or obscene. They should be True, Agreeable, and Beneficial- i.e. talk only when you want to express agreeable ideas of permanent value that will be useful to others. Do not talk unnecessarily. The energies so conserved should be channeled into chanting, reflecting, and meditating over the mantras of the scriptures. c) Mental Austerity: Serenity of mind (can be got only when the mind does not run after the sense organs and sense fields), good-heartedness (warm feeling of tender affection for all, rising from pure love), the relative silence of the mind, self-control and having pure and serene motives. Rajasic Tapas: That austerity practiced with the object of gaining power, recognition, and fame, with a hypocritical attitude is Rajasic. It cannot gather any intensity and will be unstable and impermanent. Tamasic Tapas: The austerity practiced with self-torture out of some foolish notion to destroy another is Tamasic. It leads to a disfigured, perverted, and impure personality.

5. Charity: Sattvic men do charity cheerfully, with the feeling that it has to be done as a part of his duty, without vanity or any ulterior motive, to the right person, at the right time, and right place. Rajasic men give charity reluctantly, with the hope of some return benefit, in any form or time, for the sake of pomp and show. Tamasic men give gifts egotistically, at the wrong time and place to unworthy people in an insulting way. True charity should come from within, as an urge from the heart.

The Eternal Reality: Om Tat Sat has been declared to be the triple designation of the Brahman. Om represents the Transcendental, Pure Self, upon which the Body, Mind, and

Intellect are maintained. Tat means that from which everything has come, exists, and merges back in the end. Sat means the principle of existence functioning through all things perceived, felt, and thought of in our everyday lives.

Another explanation of Om Tat Sat: is uttered when we begin acts of sacrifice, charity, and austerity. Tat indicates the Universal Truth and declares the Oneness of all living creatures. Remembering the larger interests will nullify the selfish motives and enable us to work without ego. Sat is used in the sense of Reality and Goodness and also as an auspicious act. It is also used to indicate a man's faith and devotion to sacrifice, austerity, and charity. When the chantings of OM(The Supreme), TAT(The Universal), SAT(The Real) are undertaken with faith and sincerity, the seeker's mind expands and all selfishness, ego, and arrogance disappear. All our activities are tuned up and chastened.

However diligently one may perform sacred acts, the best results are ensured only according to our motives and intentions. These can be heightened only when we detach ourselves from the material self and gain consciousness of our Spiritual Status/ Self.

Thus ends Chapter 17 of the Bhagavad Gita entitled Shraddhatrayavibhaga Yoga or The Yoga of the Three-fold Faith.

OM TAT SAT

Your Spiritual Self is the Real you

The other self is never true.

CHAPTER - 18

MOKSHA SANYASA YOGA

(The Yoga of Liberation through Renunciation {Part 1})

(Lose Your Material Self and Gain Your Spiritual Self)

This closing chapter is a summary of the entire Bhagavad Gita. Since this is a long one, it will be explained in 2 parts.

Part - 1

1. One eternal spirit functions everywhere through matter and It expresses Itself in this pluralistic world. This world is filled with innumerable people, each behaving differently, due to his unique personality. Accordingly, based on temperaments or gunas, we have three types of personalities: Pure (Sattwic), Passionate (Rajasic), and Dull (Tamasic). Each one has all three Gunas, but in different proportions. Also, the human mind and intellect function under different moods and behaviors at different times, even within the same individual. This is due to the preponderance of a particular Guna in him at a particular time. Keeping this fact clearly in mind, we should analyze ourselves constantly on why we acted/

reacted in a particular way at a particular time. This is not only a great tool for self-analysis and self discipline, but also in understanding empathetically the behavior of others. The differences in the 3 gunas about knowledge, action, doer, intelligence, fortitude, and happiness are also discussed in detail.

2. Sanyasa (Renunciation) and Tyaga (Abandonment) are the two indispensable tools for Liberation. Giving up all desire-prompted activities is Sanyasa, and performance of actions without anxieties for the fruits of the actions is Tyaga. Desire and anxiety bring about restlessness and dissipation of energy. Also, desire is always prompted by the Ego, and ONLY when the ego is eliminated, will the individual ascend to the Higher Levels. Thus, Renunciation is the goal to be reached through the process of Abandonment.

3. Tyaga (Action) is threefold- i.e. Acts of worship/sacrifice (Yagna), Charity (Daana), and Austerity (Tapas). Actions HAVE to be performed mandatorily as long as we live. Also, they become purifiers when we give up the clinging attachments and anxieties for the fruit of the actions. Sattwic Tyaga is the obligatory action done merely because it has to be done, without a sense of doership (the I-am-doing factor), without attachment or expectation of the fruits, neither hates disagreeable action nor is attached to an agreeable one. Such actions do not become binding. Rajasic Tyaga is the action performed only if it is suitable and convenient, or for egoistic purposes, or for fame and fruit, and also avoided because of fear. They deserve no merit. Tamasic Tyaga is the renouncing of obligatory duties in a deluded manner. The fruit of action in philosophy is not only its material results in this world but also the subtle constitutional changes it leaves in the thought personality of man (Vasanas) that are carried

to future births. Hence when his Vasanas are good, he returns to a joyous field of prosperity and happiness and when they are bad, to a lower strata of life. When he has a mixed Vasana, he returns to this world. All this, however, leads back to the same cycle of birth and death. The total relinquisher, free from the cycle of birth and death, will become one with the Absolute.

4. Based on the Gunas (which in turn are responsible for one's personality and natural qualities), the entire human community can be classified into 4 divisions. Brahmanas (major sattwa, little rajas, and minimum tamas), Kshatriyas(major rajas, some sattwa and tamas), Vaisyas(more rajas, less sattwa and some tamas), and Sudras (major tamas, little rajas and minimum sattwa). *These distinctions were based only on the general characteristics. However, today class distinctions have been misused, and are based on heredity or birthright alone, even without the prescribed qualities! According to a great spiritualist, in modern times, society can be divided into Creative thinkers, Politicians, Commercial Employers, and Laborers (proletarians)-.* Based on this inner equipment (gunas), the responsibilities are also different. The duties of a Brahmana are Serenity (controlling the mind from swaying into the realms of sense-enjoyments, Self Control, Tapas, Purity, Uprightness, and codes of conduct for his Spiritual life like Jnanam (knowledge), Vignanam (wisdom), and Astikyam (faith). Those of a Kshatriya include Prowess and Boldness, Fortitude, Alertness and Vigilance, Not fleeing away from battle, Generosity, and Self-confidence. The Vaisyas' duties are in the fields of Agriculture, Cattle rearing, Trade, and Commerce. The Sudras are best suited to work in a Spirit of Dedication and Service. Hence, the best course of action yielding the best results would be to carry out the duties ordained

by one's nature (swabhava), and by one's station in life (Swadharma). Then alone will one's vasanas get exhausted, and there is no chance of imprinting any new vasanas. No duty is high or low. The only condition is that it should be done in a spirit of total self-surrender, with dedication, and without any expectations. This way, work becomes worship. Thus Arjuna is advised that as he is a Kshatriya, his duty is **only** to fight, championing the cause of the good and establishing righteousness. He will **not** be doing any wrong as this is his Swabhava and Swadharma. In fact, this is the only Spiritual Sadhana for him to exhaust his existing vasanas of rajas and tamas. The Lord reiterates that running away from life and its duties is **not** Sanyasa or Renunciation. The state of Pure Awareness can be reached **only** when the prescribed activities are done selflessly, dedicatedly, without egoism, desires, and detachment from lower urges. Then alone will one be fit for meditation.

Thus ends Part 1 of the 18th chapter of the Bhagavad Gita entitled Moksha Sanyasa Yoga- Or the Yoga of Liberation through Renunciation.

OM TAT SAT

Devotion, Duty, Knowledge- through these three ways
Reach the Divine and earn His Grace.

CHAPTER - 18

MOKSHA SANYASA YOGA

(The Yoga of Liberation through Renunciation) (Part 2)

(Lose Your Material Self and Gain Your Spiritual Self)

(The first 4 points in this chapter are covered in the first part.)

5. The spiritual man is endowed with a pure intellect that is without the tendencies of acquiring, possessing, and enjoying sense objects; controlling the mind and senses with fortitude, free from likes and dislikes, eating just as much as needed, with Vairagya. Dispassion does not mean mere self-denial of any enchanting object, but a state of mind when the mind rebounds upon itself from the objects as a result of its discovery that these objects contain no real happiness. Seeking a quiet place with least disturbance, one has to steadily contemplate on the Lord. These efforts can be successful only when the deep inner personality has strong, great values.

6. Conquering Ahamkara (the feeling of ego, I-am- the-doer attitude,) is mandatory for spiritual progress. Devotion

to the Lord is NOT a mere passive surrender or a mere physical ritualism. Dissolving the ego is far more important. The 'I am the doer' mentality only gives birth to ego-centric vanities within our bosom and develops as power. This powerful ego will in turn gather more and more pride, arrogance, lust, and greed. When freed from this notion, he becomes egoless and peaceful. When constantly reinforced by definite effort and vigilance, it leads to serenity. The other aspect of the ego to be conquered is the "I am the enjoyer" mentality. Then the person is not disturbed by outward experiences and discovers a growing tranquility within himself, and can stand apart from grief and desire. Then an unfoldment takes place, whereby the veils of ignorance created by our false identification with the body drop off, and we begin to become aware of our True Self- our Divinity.

7. Integral Sadhana is the crux of the Bhagwad Gita. We need to synthesize the methods of Work (through the Body), Devotion (through the Mind), and Knowledge(through Intellect). Disciplines pursued at the body level to control the mind and turn it toward the ideal is Karma Yoga. Disciplines of channelizing emotions to control the mind and turn it toward the higher is Bhakti Yoga, and all study, reflection, detachment, and meditation practiced at the intellectual level whereby the mind is lifted to the realm of the silent experience of its own Infinitude is Jnana Yoga. All three have to be practiced in our daily lives to discipline all the three layers in us. Pursuing selfless actions, mentally surrendering them to the Supreme, and contemplating on Him is the Sure way to reach your Goal.

Thus the Lord dissects Arjuna's delusion and tells him that it is only because of his I-am-the-doer attitude (his false identification) that he has become deluded. It is The Lord alone who controls and organizes everything. His (Arjuna) job is just to do his prescribed duty as a Kshatriya, in a spirit of total surrender. He cannot run away like a coward but has to boldly face the challenges before him.

Arjuna's doubts having been dispelled and his confusion ended, he recognizes that he is but an actor who has to play his role in the drama of Life. He surrenders his ego and is now ready to take up his bow and arrow. Similarly, each one of us can recognize our True Divine Nature, which is only veiled beneath our ego-centric confusion and fears, and perform our duties in a true spirit of dedication and service. "The awakening of the Divine in us is the ending of the beast within. To discard the beast in us (sanyasa) is the liberation (Moksha) of the Divine in us", says Swami Chinmayanandaji.

Thus ends the final part of the 18th (last) chapter of the Bhagavad Gita entitled Moksha Sanyasa Yoga or the Yoga of Liberation through Renunciation.

OM TAT SAT

The Bhagavad Gita

(in a poetic format)

When on the battlefield of Kurukshetra, the chariot came in,
Arjuna saw his teachers, grandsire, kith and kin,
Down he laid his arms and, cried, "Oh No, I cannot fight !
I cannot fight, Krishna dear, turn the chariot and take flight"

Up rose Krishna, in a trice
And calmed him down with profound advice
The advice which is for all humanity
Whether past, present or the whole of eternity.

"The Atman is Pure, Immortal and Whole
No fire can burn it, no sword can slay the soul
He, you are fighting or killing is an illusion
So sway not from your path, and be not in delusion.

Life's challenges have to be met, with courage and cheer
Fight injustice, have no fear.
Do your duty without doubt or pride
And feel the fulfillment right inside.

Born in this world, act you must
Act for the general good and trust,
Eye not for fame, reward or praise
For that will mar your action's grace.

Equanimity is the key
For anyone to be free
Pleasure or pain, friend or foe
Treat them the same and see your glow.

A leaf, a flower, a fruit or just water
Offered with love and devotion pure
Is far more precious to the Master dear
Than all the riches, pomp and grandeur

Seek not for Him in temples alone
He is also there in man, plant and stone
Turn your actions to worship the Lord
Service to man too is service to God.

Three paths to tread, I give you here
Bhakti, Karma or Gynana- all are dear
Three paths to Hell, I tell you, hear
Anger, Lust and Greed- shun them now and for ever , dear.

Man is made of gunas three
Satwa, Rajas and Tamas you see
Increase the first, reduce the rest
That alone, will yield the best.

Of material desires ,do be wary
Win or lose, you'll only be sorry
Raise them instead to lofty goals
And watch how your happiness unfolds.

Devotion, faith and surrender
Is all He seeks for His Blessings to render
Look up to Him as often as you can
And perform your work as a confident man.

Arise, Awake and Stop Not, said the Lord
Fight without ego, hate or joy,
The role is assigned by the writer of the script
And He knows best, just follow the prescript.

Be off with despair, doubt and fear
Just play your part with zest and cheer
Do your duty that is Best
And leave unto the Lord, the rest".

Up then rose the Pandava bright
Gone was the thought of the coward's flight
Boldly he wielded his bow and arrow
And marched to the field devoid of sorrow.

The Bhagavad Gita is an Immortal Ocean
Drink deep from it, the Divine Potion
This Song of the Lord is the greatest teacher
Heed it well and sparkle your future.

Symbolism of The Chariot driven by 5 horses with Krishna as the charioteer

The most famous visual attached to the book of **The Bhagavad Gita** is the picture of Lord Krishna driving a chariot with 5 horses and his friend and pupil Arjuna sitting on the passenger seat.

This picture is highly symbolic, with a profound depth of spiritual meaning.

The chariot is the Sarira (body). The passenger Arjuna is the Jiva (embodied individual soul). The charioteer, is Lord Krishna, who is the Atma (the Divine Soul or the Silent Witness. sometimes also referred to as Higher Intellect or Buddhi) The horses are the Indriyas (senses, such as, eyes, ears, nose, tongue and skin.) The roads along which this chariot is driven are the objects of the senses. The reins are the operations of the Manas (Mind). Just as the reins are connected to the horses, the mind is connected to the sense organs. Analysing further, we can equate the battlefield of Kurukshetra to the constant battle within our minds. The two armies, Pandavas and Kauravas represent the Divine and Demonaic forces that constantly act upon us.

From the Kathopanishad..

The chariot stands for the human body. The five horses which draw the chariot are the five sense organs. The reins stand for the mind. and the charioteer stands for the intellect.

The rider here is the individual jiva. If the charioteer falls asleep or is not alert, then the reins which are to be controlled by the charioteer will become loose and then the horses will go out of control. This then ends up in the destruction of the chariot and the rider.

It is clear from this that if the intellect (the charioteer) loses its grip over its mind (the reins), the mind runs wherever it wants and allows the five sense organs (the five horses) to go wherever they want to and indulge. Then this brings destruction to man's personality.

Our purpose in life as human beings is to use our mind and intellect to take the chariot (body) to the ultimate destination, which is, to understand life and attain enlightenment.

OM TAT SAT.

SOME FAQs

(References : Swami Mukundanada, Swami Chinmayananda, Swami Dayananda and Swami Chidbhavananda)

1. Who is God ?

God is not a Separate entity, sitting high up in the sky. The word 'God' (and the various other names associated with the different attributes, like Goddess Lakshmi for prosperity and wealth, Parvati or Devi for power, Saraswathi for knowledge, Hanuman for valour and strength etc) is just a symbolic word for the All Pervasive Higher Force that is within and without each one of us. It is that Divine Energy or Awareness or Enlivening Force that enables the entire Cosmos to function.

2. Can 'God' be seen ?

God cannot be 'seen' in the normal sense of the term . Can the eye ever see itself ? This Divine Force can only be Realised, when our layers of ignorance are removed. For the veil of our ignorance to be removed, certain disciplines and procedures have to be undertaken and only then will the Realisation or Enlightenment happen. This is similar to boiling a vessel of milk, cooling it to room temperature, adding a spoonful of curds, setting it aside for about 8 hours, till the whole milk solidifies into curds and then finally churning the curds to realise that there is solid butter in the liquid milk !

3. When does a man become enlightened ?

When a man realises who he truly is and what is the Ultimate Truth, he becomes an enlightened soul. For the sake of easy understanding it is said that each one of us have 2 'selves' within us- The Higher Self (which is a part of Divinity Itself) and the lower self, (which consists of our gross physical body, mind and intellect). Invariably we connect ourselves with only our physical, mental and intellectual selves. " I am a beautiful, intelligent, young girl, a doctor by profession, daughter/wife/mother of so and so", etc etc...This is how we identify ourselves. We think we are this body, with (of course) a soul/atma somewhere within us. Our great masters assert that it should be the other way around. We are in Reality the Atma/Soul, carrying this human body within us. If only we learn to associate ourselves with our true Self, our Divine Nature, we will realize we are totally Whole, Pure and Complete...as enunciated by the famous verse...Om Poornamadah Poornamidham, Poornaat, Poornamudhachyate..... Hence with this Great Strength, we have to subdue the lower self and its frailties. Many enlightened souls have realized this distinction between the Self and the self (Chapter 3, Verse 43 of The Bhagavad Gita))

4. I have read that God manifests Himself in this world sometimes. Why and when does it happen ?

The Divine Principle sometimes takes on a concrete form, called as an Avatar,and descends in the world, so that mankind, with his limited power of understanding , can relate better to that Unified Entity. The biggest dharma that the individual soul can engage in is devotion to God. That is what God strengthens by taking an Avatār. When God descends in the world, he reveals his divine forms, names, virtues, pastimes, abodes, and associates. This provides the souls an easy basis for devotion. The formless aspect of God is very difficult to worship, since our mind needs a concrete form to focus on and connect with. On the other hand, devotion to the personal form of God is easy for people to comprehend, simple to perform and engage in.

When does this manifestation happen ? In Chapter 4, Verse 7 & 8 of the Gita, The Almighty says, ' Whenever there is a decline in righteousness and an increase in unrighteousness, O Arjun, at that time I manifest myself on earth'.

'To protect the righteous, to annihilate the wicked, and to reestablish the principles of dharma I appear on this earth, age after age'.

5. Where can we find the Lord ?

As explained earlier, God is not a separate entity. As He is the Subject itself and not the Object, He cannot be found. He can only be realised. But for the sake of easier understanding, 2 verses in The Gita can be quoted :

For those who see me everywhere and see all things in me, I am never lost, nor are they ever lost to me. (Chapter 6, Verse 30).

The Supreme Lord dwells in the hearts of all living beings, O Arjuna. (Chapter 18, Verse 61). The whole Universe with its diverse creations are but a projection of The One True Reality. It is the One Divinity that permeates everywhere and in everything. The Supreme Lord dwells in the heart of all beings.

6. What is the main purpose of this life ?

The main purpose of this life on earth is for us to understand the great truth that we are not just this gross physical body with a mind and intellect, but in fact a spark of the Divine Himself. The gross body only houses the Divine Self within us. And that is not all. It is the same Divinity that is present within every creation in this Universe- every human being,animal and even plants. This is True Enlightenment. We can then understand the significance of the great philosophical sayings- Tat Tvam Asi, Soham, Aham Brahmasmi. When we are able to comprehend this fact, it is easy for us to actually practice the teachings of Great Masters like Swami Vivekanand, who said that 'Service to man is Service to God, or Tagore who said that God is not found in temples, but in the hearts of men. When we thus constantly focus our mind on the Oneness of the Almighty everywhere, without being distracted by the so called plurality of this Universe,we are sure to never lose sight of Him, and consequently, neither will the Lord. This is His promise to mankind..

7. How can we reach Him ?

One can attain that total unification with the Divine, by Total Surrender. To quote from the direct text of The Gita,(Chapter 8, Verse 14, Chapter 9, V 34,)

O Parth, for those yogis who always think of Me with exclusive devotion, I am easily attainable because of their constant absorption in Me.

Always think of Me, be devoted to Me, worship Me, and offer obeisance to Me. Having dedicated your mind and body to Me, you will certainly come to me .

8. Which is the Best way to Worship the Divine ?

The Gita answers :(Chapter 9, Verses 26, 27, 30)

If one offers to Me with devotion a leaf, a flower, a fruit, or even water, I delightfully partake of that article offered with love by My devotee in pure consciousness.

Whatever you do, whatever you eat, whatever you offer as oblation to the sacred fire, whatever you bestow as a gift, and whatever austerities you perform, O son of Kunti, do them as an offering to Me.

Even if the vilest sinners worship Me with exclusive devotion, they are to be considered righteous, for they have made the proper resolve.

What lenience, what flexibility and what consideration is shown to us in order to reach Him ! No elaborate preparations, no ostentatious display, not even expensive gifts are needed. A leaf, a flower, a fruit or even simple water is sufficient for Him. All he needs is heartfelt and sincere devotion. This fact is greatly exemplified when Vidura's wife (in the Mahabharata) was so full of devotion and love when Lord Krishna came to her house, that she peeled the bananas she was offering him, threw the bananas and, absentmindedly fed Him the peels. So engrossed was she in her love for him that she did not realize this till her husband noticed it and chided her. But the Lord answered that he was happy and that his hunger was fully satisfied, as he only noticed the devotion in her and not the object.

The Lord further goes on to say that if one does not find time to devote to Him or exclusively sit and pray, it does not matter. Every action of his also can be offered as a Worship to Him. What a great solace to people who are so busy in their everyday life today! They just have to sincerely think that the work they are doing is actually their prayer to Him, and do the work to the best of their ability.

That is why, at the end of every spiritual chantings or poojas, we recite the words

kāyena vāchā manasendriyair vā buddhyātmanā vānusrita-svabhāvāt
karoti yad yat sakalam parasmai nārāyanāyeti samarpayami.

(Whatever I do) with my Body, Speech, Mind or Sense Organs, (Whatever I do) using my Intellect, Feelings of Heart or (unconsciously) through the natural tendencies of my Mind, Whatever I do, I do all for others (i.e. without the sense of attachment to the results), (And) I Surrender them all at the Lotus Feet of Sri Narayana.

9. How can I attain Peace ?

Chapter 2, V 71 gives the prescription for attaining peace.

That person, who gives up all material desires and lives free from a sense of greed, proprietorship, and egoism, attains perfect peace.

10. What are the means for the rightful way of living ?

Chapter 12 of The Gita, is the shortest (20 verses) and yet, perhaps the most important chapter to give us the prescription for the rightful way of living :

Genuine love towards all and hatred towards none which, by default, results in friendliness, compassion, empathy, and forgiveness.

Devoid of possessiveness - which automatically leads to contentment, and absence of lust, greed, aggrandizement, jealousy, attachment, anger, frustration, fear of losing and many such negative thoughts.

Equanimity of mind - trying to keep the mind balanced, whatever the situation may be. This training of the mind is something that has to be worked on very frequently and rather strictly. The mind is like a spoiled child and has to be constantly watched over and brought to the right tracks by our higher faculty- our intellect.

Absence of egoism - This is perhaps very easy to follow when we constantly reflect that by ourselves, we are Nothing! We cannot even control our own human bodies. Can we make or stop a heart beat, control the flow of the myriads of enzymes in our body, change the food we eat into energy forms that can be absorbed by the cells,or even make the blood flow in our system? Everything is controlled by a Higher Power. This realisation alone should suffice to get rid of the ' I am the Doer' attitude.

Devotion to that Higher Power, with a mind Steadfastly fixed on Him.

11. How can anyone do work without expecting any reward ?

There are many verses in The Gita that tell you the best way to do your work/action/duty - Chapter 2, Verse 47, Chapter 3 Verse 19, Chapter 18, Verse 47 etc.

You have a right to perform your prescribed duties, but you are not entitled to the fruits of your actions. Never consider yourself to be the cause of the results of your activities, nor be attached to inaction.

Therefore, giving up attachment, perform actions as a matter of duty, for by working without being attached to the fruits, one attains the Supreme.

There are 2 important points to note :1) Work is Mandatory. Having been born in this world, there is no other option than performing work. 2) Do your duty, but do not concern yourself with the results i.e without attachment to the fruit or results of your action. While the first point is readily accepted, the second point is looked upon with skepticism by most people. "How can one work without any reward or expectation" is their natural doubt. Of course this is a valid one and seems improbable. But the advice becomes very meaningful when we think a little deeper. We have the capacity to perform actions, but how do results happen ? Certainly we are not responsible for that, since the results are not dependent only upon our efforts. A number of outside factors (over which we have no control) come into play in determining the results—our efforts, destiny (our past karmas), and more importantly the judgement and views of others , competition , the cumulative karmas of the people involved, the place and situation (a matter of luck), etc. Another angle to this is, when we become anxious for results, the work will suffer. The focus is shifted from performing the action perfectly, to doubt, fear and anxiety of the result of the action. And such an action will be far from perfect. Hence the Lord advises us to focus Only on the job and perform it to the best of our ability. This is true YOGA.

12. According to The Gita, what happens to a person after death ?

(Ref. Chapter 14, 15 of The Gita) Death is nothing but a total divorce of the subtle body, (consisting of the mind and intellect along with the vasanas or latent imprints from the previous births), from its physical structure. At death, the subtle body permanently departs from the gross physical body, taking along with it the faculties or fragrance of the mind and senses, just as the wind takes the fragrance of the flowers. Thus viewed, the mind is only a bundle of vasanas (thought personality). And these vasanas can exist only in the Infinite Consciousness. Thus,the Infinite Consciousness illumining the vasanas is called the individual personality - the Jiva. This Jiva, through the equipment of the mind and senses, enjoys the objects of the world.

After departing from the physical body, the subtle body travels to the abode of the Pitrus or ancestors, called Pitruloka. After the merits gained by his good actions are exhausted, he will return to his deserved embodiments- i.e be re-born in such a situation and worthiness befitting his vasana balance. In those exceptional cases, where a person's vasana balance is NIL, and has attained Enlightenment, he will go beyond it to Brahmaloka, enjoy Bliss till the end of the cycle, and get total liberation. Thus one gets back to the world of Samsara while the other reaches Moksha- liberation.

13.Why does The Lord Himself ask Arjun to engage in the horrors of war?

The entire Bhagavad Gita consists of the advice of the Lord to Arjuna, as to why he has to fight. Two very important reasons are given. 1. It is imperative to fight against injustice and 2 It is mandatory to do one's prescribed duty, and as a Kshatriya, Arjuna's swadharma was to fight. Otherwise, it would only amount to Escapism. One has to face the challenges of life boldly and not give in to weak emotions.

14. What is the difference between the Higher Self and the lower self ?

One interpretation would be - The Higher Self refers to the All pervading Consciousness, The Brahman or The Paramatma, which is what we truly are a part of. This is our True Self. The lower self is what we normally think we are- this physical body with all its attributes, our name, profession etc. This is, in a way, our false self.

The All pervading Force or Energy is sometimes referred to as Paramatma or Consciousness which is the enlivening factor of all Creation. It is also called Purusha. When a spark of this Purusha gets embodied in physical matter, consisting of the 5 elements, sensory organs, mind intellect, ego etc, called Prakriti, it gives rise to an individual, called Jiva (Jivatma)- an individual soul. (Chapter 13 - Kshetra Kshetrajna Yoga of The Gita, deals with this elaborately).

15. What is Spirituality ?

The term Spirituality is highly misunderstood. It is often associated with the eighty and above age groups or the sages, saints and monks ! Spirituality is nothing but connecting yourself to a Higher reality, which could be either religious deities, one's own Higher Self, Nature, Love and Devotion and Service to the needy, one's duties, and so on. To Swami Ramakrishna Paramhansa it was Goddess KaliMa, to Mother Teresa , it was Love and Service to the poor and needy, to the poet William Wordsworth, it was Nature.... And so on. Practices like Contemplation on one's Higher Self, Prayer, Meditation, Love of Nature, Yoga- all help one to become more Spiritual. It has great benefits including removal of stress and negativity in one's life, and an overall well being.

OM TAT SAT.

OM TAT SAT

("Om Tat Sat" is a sacred mantra and declaration that symbolizes the ultimate reality and Brahman. Aum: Represents the unmanifest invisible realm, the primordial sound, and the vibratory power of God. Tat: Means "Brahman". Sat: Means "the ultimate reality." The phrase is said to help people awaken to their true nature, and to remind them that they are more than just a body and mind.)

AN IMPORTANT NOTE TO THE READER

This summary of the Great Gospel The Bhagavad Gita, is just an eye-opener. It is but a small drop gleaned out from the Ocean of the marvelous text. It is simply a pointer, giving some points from the Revered Scripture. I have hardly touched the tip of the iceberg. Even so, this cannot be read in one go, or in a hurried manner. It is to be read and re-read, at a slow pace, and pondered over, with full faith and devotion. Many of the points may seem idealistic and even impractical. But, please do not be judgemental and dismiss them. They are invaluable, precious gems, handed down to us through centuries. Whenever you feel you need more clarifications please refer to the wonderful commentaries written by our great sages and saints like Swami Chinmayanada, Swami Tapasyananda, Paramahansa Yogananda, Swami Mukundananda, etc.

Let us resolve to keep our tryst with the Bhagavad Gita on a continual, perpetual basis. We may not suddenly become 'realized souls' but we will have surely started on this great journey of Realization. Remember the promise of the Lord Himself: 'No Spiritual practice Ever goes in vain'!

Wish you all an enlightening reading/listening and may the Blessings of the Almighty be showered upon all of us, enabling us to lead our lives the Gita Way.

I conclude with the customary offering of this endeavor to the Almighty.

yat karosi yad asnasi yaj juhosi dadasi yat
yat tapasyasi kaunteya tat kurusva mad-arpanam

(Whatever I do either by body, speech, mind, or sensory organs, either with my personal knowledge or natural trait, I surrender and submit all, to that supreme divine Narayana.)

HARI OM TAT SAT